DELIVER ON YOUR PROMISE

How Simulation-Based Scheduling Will Change Your Business

C. Dennis Pegden, Ph.D.

Table of Contents

Preface

You're a manager. You may be in charge of a make-to-order product, or maybe you oversee transportation and logistics in the service industry. But no matter what you do, the most important part of your job is to make your customers happy. And your biggest headache? It's scheduling, and all the ugly words that so often come with it: long lead times, late orders, overtime hours, high production costs—and unhappy customers.

Many companies, possibly the one you work for, have already invested in information systems to try and ease the whole scheduling process. Enterprise Resource Planning (ERP), for example, or Advanced Planning and Scheduling (APS) systems can track customer orders, plan production, and order materials. And more complex Manufacturing Execution Systems (MES) can tell you the status of the production floor and the flow of work through your system. These various tools can help with things like ordering during specific planning periods, providing information on individual pieces of equipment, and knowing the whereabouts of each order on the factory floor.

Yet while these planning and tracking systems often promise headache-free automation, they're ultimately limited for a simple reason: they aren't designed to actually transform your company's production plan into a detailed and reliable schedule. Therefore, those of you in charge of scheduling still have to use—or eventually revert back to using—tedious manual methods. Armed with little more than a spreadsheet, a planning board, and copious amounts of coffee, you can put in hours of work on a schedule but still aren't guaranteed success. And when a machine breaks down on the factory floor or one supplier misses a deadline? Well, your schedule becomes obsolete and your production staff often ends up reacting to those situations without having a clear overview of the big picture.

What is ultimately lacking in the ERP/APS and the MES systems is the ability

(1) to model accurately the precise details in your system, and (2) to deal with the inevitable risks and uncertainties within that system. This first issue creates schedules that are non-actionable in real life, while the second results in overly optimistic schedules that lead you to make promises you can't keep. Either way, you end up not meeting desired KPIs, profit margins decline, and customers aren't happy. Bring on the headache.

So what's missing in this critical chain of events in your business? Risk-based Planning and Scheduling (RPS) addresses both of these problems and results in a real-time schedule that fully accounts for all the moving elements of your company's production. This book was written to lay out the key problems with the current approach to scheduling and to show you the benefits of transitioning to a system that can generate a dynamic, interactive, simulated production schedule. And as an added bonus, reading it will help you take stock of your company, re-envision resources to improve profitability, and understand how scheduling directly impacts what you can promise your customers.

We can help you deliver on that promise.

The Current State of Scheduling

CHAPTER 1

How Great Scheduling Gives You a Competitive Edge

With the globalization of manufacturing and the continuing shift from a make-to-stock to a make-to-order manufacturing environment, scheduling has become critically important. There's no doubt that in today's world, companies compete not only on quality and price, but also on their ability to deliver products and services reliably and on time. A good schedule, therefore, determines a company's sales, their on-time delivery performance, and their customer satisfaction ratings. And because scheduling defines the limit to throughput, that schedule also establishes the revenue that can be ultimately generated by a company. All of this drives short-term issues (such as overtime) to meet customer demands, as well as long-term investments (like additional equipment). Scheduling, then, is really the key driver for the metrics that define cash flow, return on investment, and ultimately the success of a company.

This chapter provides a quick explanation of how good scheduling helps your business deliver a quality product—reliably and at the lowest cost—in order to optimize profitability and keep your customers happy.

Planning vs. Scheduling

Let's start by making a clear distinction between planning and scheduling. Planning is the high-level process of identifying what work needs to be done and what materials are required to perform that work, and it involves strategy about what to produce at each facility during each production period. Planning is typically done in the context of time buckets (such as weeks or months) and can be determined without any detailed model of your company's system.

Scheduling, on the other hand, turns this top-level plan into a detailed, actionable, reliable timetable so your company can produce required items and meet key objectives—including on-time delivery. Scheduling focuses on the intense, short-term contention for both production resources and materials, and it requires you to fully understand every critical variable and constraint within your system.

Smart planning is an absolute prerequisite for scheduling. And smart scheduling is what allows you to put your best plans into action. Planning and scheduling are therefore interdependent, and require a full understanding of all of your company's moving parts.

When is Scheduling Most Important?

Scheduling provides its biggest competitive edge when one or more of the following conditions are present:

* In a make-to-order environment, where orders are produced to meet demand for a specific customer, rather than a simple make-to-stock situation.
* In a more complex make-to-stock environment that produces multiple products with significant changeovers, resulting in production sequences that significantly impact throughput.
* When on-time delivery to customers is a key performance indicator.
* When the production process is expensive and, as a result, you have a resource-constrained system with orders that compete for plant capacity.
* In situations you're making multiple products at the same time, and each product flows differently through the system.
* When unplanned but likely disruptions—such as machine breakdowns and late material arrivals—require rescheduling.

Scheduling doesn't provide a considerable competitive edge in the relatively simple straight-line production of a single product (like most assembly lines) because such items are produced on a continuous basis. Simulation and other process improvements can still maximize throughput in such straight-line systems, however, and can also add significant value to suppliers that feed component parts to these straight lines.

The Basics on Buffers

For companies modeled on make-to-stock items, manufacturing problems and inefficiencies can be buffered by inventory stored in warehouses. Production efforts focus on maximizing throughput to resupply this inventory, and while this adds cost and an element of inflexibility, customer demand can be met simply by pulling products from available stock.

In today's more common make-to-order environment, however, this inventory buffer is gone. To make on-time deliveries, then, manufacturers turn to a capacity buffer to address short periods of demand for certain resources. This results in lengthy idle periods for expensive machines—just in case they are needed to meet short-term demand—so just-in-time (JIT) inventory is replaced with a just-in-case (JIC) increase in capacity. Like the inventory buffer, this capacity buffer adds unnecessary cost to the system.

When the capacity buffer is inadequate or too expensive to meet demand, the next buffer is time. In this case, lead times are increased based on competition for limited resources, but this often results in unhappy customers and lost sales. Companies can resort to overtime or may choose to invest in extra equipment to improve these lead times, but it all boils down to one question: What is the smartest use of resources? And this, of course, circles back to the critical need for good scheduling.

Rather than adding cost to any system—whether it's through inventory, capacity, or time buffering—the priority should be to reduce variability and to optimize the use of existing resources, which is all possible through better scheduling. The next chapter dissects the scheduling systems many companies currently rely on, and shows what these systems can—and cannot—do.

Good scheduling makes the best use of available resources, thus reducing a reliance on buffers and saving money. In short, scheduling keeps all the gears of your company running smoothly.

▶

....

CHAPTER 2

Making Sense of the Alphabet Soup

What ERP, MES, APS, and SCADA Systems Do

Most enterprises—and likely your company—use an information system to help with planning and scheduling. These systems date back to the 1960's when a man named Joe Orlicky developed a model known as Material Requirements Planning, or MRP. (Oh, and just in case you're interested, Black & Decker became the first company to use it in 1964.) These original MRP systems focused on planning production, with a central goal of being able to track materials and requirements through a system. MRP II systems added more functions, including capabilities like demand forecasting and rough-cut capacity planning. And then more modern Enterprise Resource Planning systems (ERP), led by the SAP company, combined all of the MRP II features with accounting, human resources, and other functions to make an integrated IT system. And finally, ERP systems added Supply Chain Management (SCM) to control inventory and distribution.

These MRP/ERP systems have two primary outputs for managing production. The first is a master list of production orders—such as release dates, due dates, and order quantities—along with end products and component products required

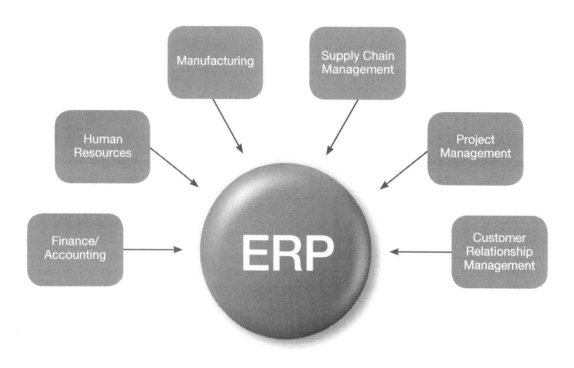

Figure 1: An Enterprise Resource Planning system can help a company coordinate materials with production.

during production. The second output is a purchasing schedule that lists items required from outside suppliers, including their expected arrival time, with the goal of matching these materials up to the production schedule. Taken together, these two outputs help a company with aspects like viewing material requirements across orders, determining production lot sizes, and planning for quantities for purchased materials. Figure 1 shows how an MRP/ERP coordinates materials with production to ensure the essential "what," "when," and "how much" of a process.

Costs and drawbacks to MRP/ERP systems

Widely deployed in businesses, MRP/ERP systems are expensive to install and maintain. It's not uncommon for a Global 2000 company to spend $100 million for a system, take years to fully implement it, and then have to spend another $50 million on upgrades to keep the system current. Even mid-sized companies can spend $10 to $20 million to implement a system. Are they worth the cost?

Two of the key drawbacks in the MRP/ERP systems are the assumptions they make when generating any master schedule. The first assumption is that every product included in the schedule has a known and fixed lead time, one that will remain independent of current or future congestion on the factory floor. This fixed lead time is subsequently used in the process of backward scheduling to determine release dates based on due dates. In most cases, a time bucket or planning period consolidates all jobs within the planning period to start at the same time, and all material is assumed to be required at the beginning of this planning period.

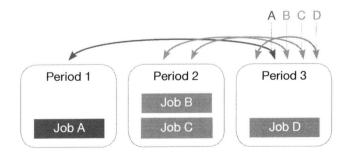

Figure 2: Four jobs (A, B, C, and D) scheduled backward using fixed lead time and three time buckets. Vertical lines mark due dates and reverse arrows are lead times.

Did you see in Figure 2 how all jobs are assumed to start at the beginning of each time bucket? And that there's no specific sequence for how the jobs should be performed? This is just an example of how a schedule can look clean, clear, and simple on paper but doesn't actually help you in the real world.

The second simplifying assumption made by MRP/ERP systems is that a factory has an infinite capacity to produce whatever is scheduled during that planning period. In our illustration above, jobs B and C are both scheduled into the second time bucket with no consideration for whether there's enough capacity to produce both jobs concurrently. And again, there's no plan for how the jobs should be sequenced to complete them on time. Some MRP/ERP systems have added modules to do rough-cut capacity planning to address this infinite capacity assumption, but the true constraints of the system are largely ignored.

Neither of these assumptions—fixed lead times or infinite capacity—is accurate, of course. It's not at all uncommon for actual lead times to vary dramatically from the ERPs fixed lead time, or for a job to waste more than 95% of its time idle, limited by constraints like equipment or workers. But these assumptions are required to simplify the calculations performed by the MRP/ERP systems.

More abbreviation: APS, MES, and SCADA

Advanced Planning and Scheduling systems (APS)—which are also sometimes called Advanced Planning and Optimization (APO)—can provide master planning, additional supply chain management, and scheduling capabilities to the ERP system. But again, because these systems must make simplified assumptions about production in order to crunch certain numbers, they're limited in their ability to formulate a reliable, actionable schedule.

Finally, while the MRP/ERP system takes a broad forward-looking view of the production process, a Manufacturing Execution System (MES) can track the transformation of raw materials into finished products by looking at what's happening on the factory floor, and then offer a detailed record of all actions that have taken place within the production system. The MES also expands on the MRP/ERP systems by sending alerts when processes fall outside of set limits, and it can ultimately help with the analysis of the throughput. MES systems—

including a product like Wonderware—provide a connection between the MRP/ERP system and the Supervisory Control and Data Acquisition (SCADA) system, which uses programmable logic controllers (PLCs) to interface with all of the equipment in the facility.

In an attempt to organize this confusing "alphabet soup," the following visual shows the relationships between the initial stages of a job—where a planner thoughtfully outlines what is desirable—to the final stages when information is captured on the successful operational aspects of that job. But what is the key element in the middle? Actionable and reliable scheduling.

Earlier in this chapter, we said how the early stages of planning are dedicated to thinking about a problem in order to determine "what," "when," and "how much." And skipping to the end of the process, after the problem has been solved, it proves invaluable to have a record of the whole operation. But it's the scheduling in the middle—the actionable "how" of things—that requires critical attention. And unfortunately, because it's so often left to imperfect assumptions and uncontrolled variables, scheduling becomes the missing link in the chain of events.

Before discussing a solution, we're going to take a little more time to define the problem by identifying the scheduling variables that cause the biggest headaches, clarifying the difference between infinite and finite scheduling, and looking at the three most common approaches to scheduling.

Figure 3: Scheduling sits between planning and execution.

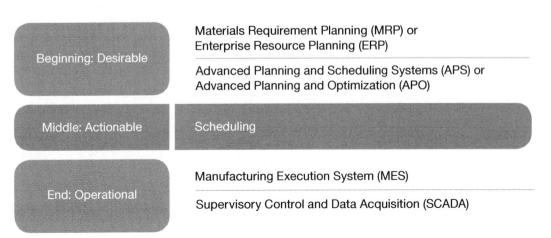

▶

....

CHAPTER 3

Why is Scheduling So Difficult?

Feasibility, Variation, and What Can Go Wrong

As mentioned in the previous chapter, planning for any kind of production or logistical operation begins with a wide view of what needs to be accomplished. Scheduling is the next necessary step in order to put that master plan into action. Good scheduling requires a study of the details (available workers, equipment, production processes, and other variables) in order to function in real time, but ERP systems with scheduling capabilities must reduce or simplify complexities in order to crunch their numbers. Simplifying means making default assumptions, and two assumptions in particular—that jobs have fixed lead times and that a facility has an infinite capacity—can result in some very unreliable, headache-inducing schedules.

After investing heavily in information systems like ERP and MES, why is the element of scheduling still so difficult? Why are some enterprises still resorting to tedious manual methods? Why is it all such a struggle?

Scheduling is ($N!^M$) hard!

The first thing to acknowledge is that scheduling truly is a complex issue. In fact, scheduling problems are formally classified within computational mathematics as NP-hard (short for non-deterministic polynomial-time hard). Without getting into too much mathematical detail, NP-hard falls into the category of the most complex computational problems, where computation time explodes as the size of the problem increases. As a result, there are no algorithms that can provide a guaranteed optimal solution in a reasonable amount of time.

The computational complexity of scheduling derives from the explosive combinatorial nature of the problem. To illustrate, consider a simple manufacturing system comprised of N (jobs) and M (machines). Figure 4 shows that if we have two jobs and two machines, where each job must visit each machine once, the result is fairly simple: there are four possible options.

But in Figure 5, we increase N and M—meaning that as many as six jobs each need to visit three machines once—and the number of combinations absolutely explodes, shown in math using "!" as the factorial symbol: $N!^M$. And keep in mind that in real systems, it's not unusual to have thousands of jobs and hundreds of machines, leading to an enormous number of possible schedules to consider.

Even though marketing materials for some scheduling tools claim to be able to generate an optimal schedule, can you now understand why none can actually do that? All of the tools use some type of heuristics to generate a scheduling solution, so what the marketers should say is, "Although this schedule is likely sub-optimal, it's hopefully better than what a human can do using a spreadsheet."

Focusing on what's feasible and finite

What is necessary for better scheduling in this difficult environment is an understanding of the limits and constraints in the system so that all resources can be explicitly considered, and so that processes—especially concurrent ones—can be sequenced correctly. These constraints can be represented using mathematical expressions, or they can be modeled through simulation. But regardless of the approach, tools that are based on constraints in a system are referred to as Finite Capacity Scheduling tools, or FCS.

Figure 4: *Four possible schedules with two jobs and two machines.*

Option	Machine A	Machine B
1	Job 1 then Job 2	Job 1 then Job 2
2	Job 1 then Job 2	Job 2 then Job 1
3	Job 2 then Job 1	Job 1 then Job 2
4	Job 2 then Job 1	Job 2 then Job 1

Figure 5: *The number of schedules explodes as the number of jobs and machines increases.*

Number of Jobs	Number of Machines	Number of Schedules
3	3	216
4	3	13,000
5	3	1,700,000
6	3	373,000,000

The output from FCS tools is a detailed schedule for the flow of work through the system, including the times at which each operation will start, the material that will be consumed/produced, the equipment that will be used and in what sequence, and the workers that will be assigned to each task. While the ERP focuses on demand and material, the FCS adds the third critical element of capacity and then considers all three of these elements simultaneously.

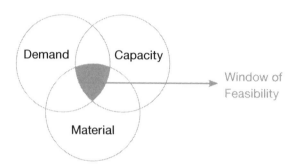

The schedule generated by FCS tools is essentially the window of feasibility at the center of these three elements. And in more complex environments, this window can shrink even smaller because of how all the components must interact. This all works to prove that, in order to ensure feasible scheduling, it's critical to have a detailed constraint model that recognizes each and every activity that influences the outcome of your planning.

The Gantt chart and its uses

Records show that Polish businessman Karol Adamiecki first conceived of a way to graphically represent a schedule in 1896, referring to it as a *harmonogram* (from the Greek *harmonia* "agreement" and *gramma* "that which is drawn"). But it was an American mechanical engineer named Henry Gantt who popularized the business tool in the 1910s. What a Gantt chart does is display time bars across a timeline, where the length of the bar represents the duration of an activity. Each row in a "resource" Gantt chart, for example, is a specific resource with time bars showing specific steps for each job being processed. Each row in a "job" or "entity" Gantt chart, on the other hand, denotes a specific job or order, and the time bars are the resources that are required to process that entity.

Figure 6

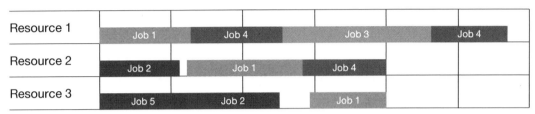

Resource Gantt Chart: Five jobs being processed along three resources. For example, Job 1 is being processed first on Resource 1, then Resource 2, and then Resource 3.

Figure 7

Timeline

Job 1	Resource 1	Resource 2	Resource 3			
Job 2	Resource 2	Resource 3				
Job 3			Resource 1			
Job 4		Resource 1		Resource 2		Resource 1
Job 5	Resource 3					

Job Gantt Chart: These are the same five jobs and three resources from the Resource Gantt Chart above, but here the jobs run horizontally across the chart to show how they're being processed through the resources.

When finite capacity scheduling is performed in a scheduler-in-the-loop mode, the schedule is generated and displayed to the scheduler using Gantt charts and other reports. The scheduler can then manipulate the schedule—by dragging and dropping jobs on the Gantt—before committing the schedule to production and distributing paper or electronic reports. This approach is most useful when the constraint model being used is a simplified representation of the actual system, and then a human scheduler adjusts it before it becomes actionable. [See Figure 8]

Some finite capacity scheduling is integrated into the ERP and MES system as a "solver," with no human intervention. Each time a significant change occurs on the factory floor (like machine breaking down), a new schedule is automatically generated and published for everyone affected. This second mode of operation requires a more detailed constraint model so it can produce actionable schedules that don't require human review and adjustment. [See Figure 9]

The basics of variability

Understanding the impact of variability in scheduling is the least intuitive challenge, and cruelly, the one most responsible for the complexity of scheduling solutions. In the terminology of Lean Manufacturing, variability is equated to the Japanese word *muda*, meaning "futility or wastefulness" because, as a rule, increasing variability always decreases performance.

Although the effects of variation may seem small enough to ignore when examining an individual task, the cumulative impact of variations across many tasks can have a dramatic impact on the system performance. This illustration shows a very simple system where we have jobs—represented by green triangles—arriving and waiting their turn to be processed by a single server:

Waiting Line   Server

Figure 8: The human scheduler may need to adjust a schedule to make it actionable.

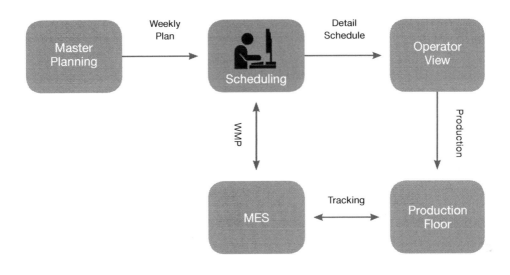

Figure 9: The scheduling system produces actionable schedules with no human interaction.

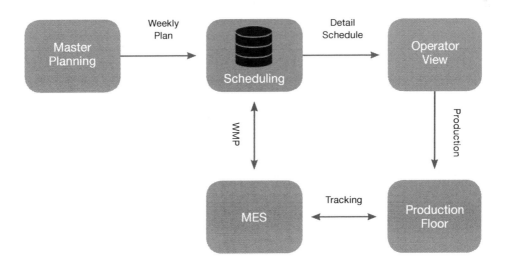

Figure 10

	Variability		Waiting Time
	Arrivals	Processing	Hours
1	No	No	0
2	Yes	No	5
3	No	Yes	5
4	Yes	Yes	10

Adding variability—in this example based on the exponential distribution—to either the arrival or processing time adds 5 hours of waiting time. Variation in the arrival and processing time would then contribute equally to a 10-hour wait.

Figure 11

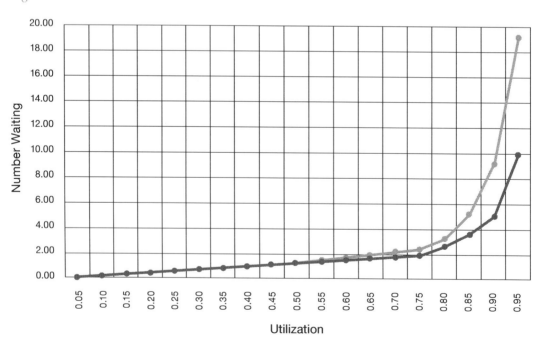

The lower line is for variation in the arrival process, while the upper line indicates variation in both arrival and processing.

The average time between arrivals is 60 minutes, and the average processing time is 55 minutes. From basic calculations, we know that our server should be busy 91.7% of the time and have a 5-minute break between jobs. If the system is deterministic (meaning it has no variability), then jobs have zero waiting time. Each job arrives to an idle server, is processed for 55 minutes, and then 5 minutes later the next job arrives.

Now let's consider what happens when we add variability to the system. The table on the facing page summarizes the waiting time in the queue for four different scenarios: (1) no variability, (2) variability in the arrivals only, (3) variability in the processing time only, and (4) variability in both the arrival process and the processing time.

What would happen if we invested in a second server for the fourth scenario? Well, we could reduce the waiting time to 16 minutes. But if we had two options—to either eliminate variability from the system or to invest in a second server—we are better off keeping a single server (incurring no additional investment), and eliminating the variability. Although this example is very simple, it shows the degrading role that variation has on any system. It also illustrates the folly of focusing strictly on utilization during system design as a KPI for the system performance. In the presence of variability, it's not possible to have high utilization without also incurring long waiting times and excessive work in process. The capacity buffer, therefore, is the price that must be paid to have short wait times and low work in process in the presence of variability. The graph on the facing page shows how the number waiting in our small example explodes as a function of utilization. The key takeaway is how the presence of variation requires a management tradeoff between carrying excess capacity (low utilization) and high work-in-process.

What happens when—not if—things go wrong

Variation impacts both the long- and short-term behavior of any system, and therefore has a direct impact on scheduling. Using deterministic scheduling produces a "happy" path that assumes everything goes as expected, just as we concluded a zero-waiting time in the previous example. The role this kind of variation plays in creating congestion and delays in manufacturing is well documented in the literature, but it's typically ignored in the day-to-day planning and scheduling of production. Advanced Planning and Scheduling (APS) tools have to ignore variation in order to generate schedules, and in some cases, it takes hours of computation to generate these unreliable and unrealistic schedules!

Let's illustrate this point by taking a simple scheduling problem comprised of a single machine. Look below at Figure 12. It shows how jobs arrive to this machine every hour, and each requires 55 minutes to process. They can then be picked up two hours after they arrive, so this Gantt chart provides a look at a simple deterministic schedule for processing the first three jobs.

This schedule looks fine. We have 91.7% utilization of our machine, a 5-minute break between each 55-minute job, and all jobs have a 65-minute slack time between their planned completion time and their due date (indicated by the dashed line) built into the schedule. Because we have a slack that exceeds our makespan to buffer unforeseen problems, this looks to be a robust schedule for our three planned jobs upon initial inspection.

Systems in real life, however, have a way of throwing out many sources of variations. Processing times typically vary from job to job. Or purchased components arrive late and hold up the start of an operation. Machines break down and require new parts. Or a member of the crew may not show up for work. These variables are often beyond our control, yet they degrade the schedule and cause our performance to fall far short of our careful plans.

Figure 12: The deterministic schedule appears to be fine.

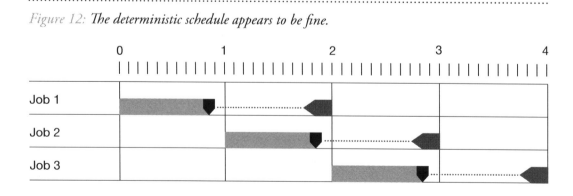

What really happens, then, to the long-term behavior of that robust-looking schedule? We'll now assume that our data represents expected values, and the actual times vary around these values. To simplify the mathematical analysis, we'll make the common assumption that both the time between job arrivals and the processing time on the machine are exponentially distributed, so we can use basic queuing theory to compute the long-term behavior for scheduling on this single machine.

With these variations factored into our system, a simple queuing analysis shows that in reality, our system performs very poorly. While our long-term machine utilization remains 91.7%, our machine usage is highly variable. The machine operator is frequently working long periods without a break, and at other times is starved for work with long periods of idleness. Each arriving job waits an average of 10 hours before it starts processing, and only 16% of our orders are ready on time. We have the same physical capacity and average times as before, except our inventory levels and on-time performance are terrible. What appears to be a good and feasible plan based on deterministic values becomes unmanageable when variation is considered.

Need an aspirin yet?

This example may illustrate, all too familiarly, why there's such a gap between the promises of existing APS tools and the reality of how scheduling works in a complex system filled with variation and uncertainty. Schedules generated by deterministic tools can't properly deal with the realities of the factory floor, and even small variations in activity behavior result in large variations in the overall system response. Because of the critical role that variation plays in system performance, reducing variation is a primary focus of process improvement initiatives.

In the first few chapters of this book, we've addressed scheduling problems and the variety of solutions companies have implemented to try and solve these frustrating problems. But in the following chapter, the final one in this section, we want to provide a summary of the three of the most common approaches to scheduling to clarify underlying issues and place all of this in a real-world context.

CHAPTER 4

The Three Most Common Approaches to Scheduling

Now that we've established the importance of good scheduling—and its confounding complexities—let's go through the three most common approaches to solving the scheduling issue in use today: (1) manual scheduling using planning boards or spreadsheets, (2) constraint-based scheduling using solvers, and (3) simulation-based scheduling approaches using first-generation programs.

Manual Scheduling

The manual scheduling approach remains in wide use today, which means that in many companies, the constraint model exists in the head of the scheduler. (If this is you, feel free to substitute the pronouns "I" every time we mention "the scheduler. This may put more pressure on you, however, so we apologize.) The scheduler must have a commanding knowledge of the system to manually generate an actionable schedule, one that fully respects the constraints in the system. The feasibility and quality of the schedule—which is often completed on an erasable white board or using a spreadsheet—is therefore determined entirely by how much experience and skill the scheduler has.

Relying on their fund of knowledge of the system, the scheduler must sequence the work across the resources, and in complex systems, this requires taking many factors into consideration: tooling, worker skill sets, travel time, material requirement, sequence-dependent changeovers, etc. Schedulers sometimes rely on spreadsheet tools, such as Excel or other templates, to assist with a rough starting schedule for further manipulation.

Although the manual approach to scheduling may be just fine for very simple processes, it puts companies at a competitive disadvantage in typical high-dynamic production systems. Five of the most frustrating drawbacks include:

* Manual scheduling typically takes hours to complete, and the moment any change occurs, that hard-earned schedule becomes invalid. Without an actionable schedule, production staff is often left to make local decisions without knowing how these decisions impact the system KPIs.

* It's difficult for the scheduler to consider all the critical constraints in a complex system. While schedulers can typically focus on primary constraints, they are often unaware—or must ignore—secondary constraints, and these omissions lead to a non-actionable schedule.

* The quality of a manual schedule is entirely dependent on the scheduler. If he or she retires or is out for vacation or illness, the backup scheduler may be less skilled and KPIs may degrade.

* It's essentially impossible for the scheduler to account for the degrading effect of variation on the schedule and thus provide confident completion times for orders. This typically results in schedules that are optimistic and overpromise on delivery, or else they lead to extra-long time buffers that result in unhappy customers.

* As critical jobs become late, manual schedulers resort to bumping other jobs for these "hot" jobs, disrupting the flow and forcing more "hot" jobs. The system becomes jerky because it's constantly responding to customer complaints about late orders, and scheduling devolves into little more than firefighting.

By eliminating the tedious and time-consuming task of generating a manual schedule, the scheduler would have more time to focus on activities that directly impact delivery performance. This may include having time to analyze potential changes (such as expediting materials, adding overtime, or delaying optional maintenance) in order to enhance KPI performance and lower the delivery risk for critical jobs.

Manual scheduling requires minimal investment in technology and is therefore often the default method for companies that have failed to find and implement a good solution to their scheduling problem. Companies that have invested in ERP and MES systems but still use a manual scheduling approach have an opportunity to make significant competitive improvements through better scheduling.

By eliminating the frustrating and time-consuming aspects of manual scheduling, a scheduler has considerably more time to focus on the kinds of activities that directly impact delivery performance.

Constraint-based Scheduling

With the constraint-based scheduling approach, scheduling is formulated as a set of mathematical constraints that must be satisfied to meet an objective (such as minimizing late jobs, or maximizing throughput). The mathematical formulation is then "solved" using a Constraint Programming (CP) heuristic algorithm, sometimes called a CP solver. The CP solver uses heuristic rules to search for candidate solutions that satisfy the constraints and improve the objective.

An example of this approach is scheduling solutions based on the i2 Factory Planner, the IBM ILOG CPLEX CP Optimizer, or the SAP APO-PP/DS module. This approach can work well for small applications with minimal complexity. But people can be misled by the reference to the term "optimizer" or "solver" in these constraint-based approaches, believing the resulting solution will be better than other methods. As we discussed in the previous chapter, however, the scheduling problem is NP-hard and there is no solver that can generate a guaranteed optimal solution. Because of the limitations of the constraint-based approach, these systems sometimes augment the constraint-based approach with simple scheduling heuristics to provide an alternative way to generate a solution. And some installations of the SAP APO PP/DS module make no use of the constraint "optimizer" and rely exclusively on the simple scheduling heuristics to generate a solution.

The limitations of constraint-based scheduling include:

* They are deterministic, meaning they ignore variation and omit key aspects in order to keep the size and complexity manageable for the CP solver. This leads to overly optimistic and non-actionable schedules.

* They require a long time to generate a solution. Indeed, a maximum computation time is typically specified and the best schedule that can be found within the time is accepted.

* The form of these constraints is limited and depending upon the system being scheduled, it may be difficult or impossible to create an underlying constraint model that is sufficiently accurate to produce actionable schedules.

* It's difficult to communicate and visualize the constraint model in these systems. The model is in the form of mathematical equations, or the computer

code that represents these equations. Hence, only a few people—if any—in the organization can view and understand the model.

These challenges have resulted in a relatively low success rate for constraint-based scheduling solutions. Simply stated, they often fail to truly help your company with reliable scheduling and are very expensive to implement.

Simulation-based scheduling

Simulation-based scheduling relies on a simulation model to provide the underlying constraint model for the system. The simulation model captures all resources (including elements like equipment, tools, and workers) as well as the materials that are consumed and produced in the process. A schedule can then be generated by simulating the flow of jobs through a model of the system, and resource and material usage can be recorded from workstation to workstation within the model. The quality of the resulting schedule is driven by the heuristic decision rules that are embedded into the model.

As an example of a heuristic decision rule, a simulation-based schedule may use a minimum changeover requirement to select the next job to process at a workstation. This rule examines all available jobs and selects the job that requires the least changeover from the previous one. These tools provide a range of heuristic scheduling rules to generate schedules that focus on some combination of maximizing throughput or minimizing late orders. A schedule generated by the simulation mimics the actual flow of work that occurs in the facility whenever these same heuristic rules are applied. While the previous two sections listed detriments of manual scheduling and constraint-based scheduling, here's a list of the benefits of simulation-based schedule:

* Simulation allows the system to incorporate complex decision logic for selecting the next job to process or the resources to allocate to a job.
* Any of the standard dispatching rules used in production such as minimizing setup, critical ratio, etc. can be selected to optimize the scheduling performance.
* Whenever an event occurs that alters the workflow (a machine breaks down, required materials have not arrived, or a worker is not present) the system can

handle the changing dynamics and quickly generate a new schedule.

- Campaign rules (for example, light to dark or thin to thick) or composite rules that combine multiple strategies are also easy to implement. This means simulation can support the idea of custom decision rules for specific applications, allowing these decisions to leverage the experience and skills of the human operator.

Solving the NP-Hard Problem: Comparing Heuristic Approaches

We'd like to take a minute here to point out that the constraint-based and simulation-based approaches to scheduling tackle the unsolvable NP-Hard problem in very different ways. In the constraint-based approach, the problem is formulated as a set of mathematical relationships, and then a heuristic solver is applied to search for a solution that satisfies constraints. Even when one is found, the solver continues to search, trying to improve on that solution. Because the heuristic solver is not guaranteed to find a solution, and a solution may take significant time, the trade-off is to keep the constraint set overly simplified and even ignore potentially important constraints in order to create a problem that isn't too hard for the solver.

In contrast, the simulation-based approach allows us to create a simulation model of the system, and we are free to add as many constraints and as much detail as necessary. In place of the solver, we simulate the flow of work through the model based on resource, material, sequencing, and other constraints just as it would occur in the real system. Improvements in the schedule result from the implementation of smart-decision heuristics within the model: which item to process next on a machine, for example, or which resources to assign to a specific task. The schedule is quickly constructed in a single run of the simulation model, and there's no need to trade off the complexity of the constraints in order to get a solution in a reasonable time.

To summarize, the constraint-based approach requires a search for a solution to a set of equations, whereas the simulation-based approach constructs a solution by simulating the flow of work through a model of the system. While the simulation-based case still uses heuristics, those heuristics are very specific and are used to make important scheduling decisions as the simulation model is executed.

Let's describe scheduling in a nutshell…

The basic challenges of scheduling come down to three things: having an accurate model representation, reducing computation time to generate a schedule, and having clear communication and visualization of the model and the schedule. Let's consider each of these three features and how they relate to scheduling options overall.

The first key feature is the model representation. As with any complex problem, we rely on a model to schedule our system. In the case of a manual scheduling approach this is a mental model of the system, whereas computer-based approaches produce a computer model. For the computer model to be useful, it must represent the actual system in enough detail to produce a valid output in terms of an actionable schedule. Since the typical system is complex and may have unique operating constraints, the modeling framework must be very flexible and customizable. Ultimately, the model must accurately capture the complexity and uniqueness of the system, as well as the variability in the system.

The second key feature is computation time, meaning how long it takes to generate a new schedule. In most organizations, the useful life of a schedule is short because unplanned events always occur that make the current schedule invalid. A new schedule must be considered, regenerated, and distributed to the organization as immediately as possible. It may help here to compare the capabilities of simulation to the assistance of Google maps when driving. These "living maps" devise a route to a destination and announce step-by-step directions to the driver. And when— either by choice or by mistake—the driver makes a turn that wasn't suggested, the system recalculates to find a new route, adjusting further directions and arrival times accordingly. If Google's system cannot regenerate another reliable route within seconds, the driver is frustrated and lost. And if an actionable schedule cannot be refreshed? Then an organization can quickly spiral down with reactive, uncommunicated actions.

The final key feature is the ease of communicating and visualizing both the model structure and the schedule results. A shared understanding of the constraint model throughout the organization is essential for building confidence about the soundness and quality of the resulting schedules. Ideally, anyone in

The basic challenges of scheduling dictate the desired features of a scheduling solution: (1) an accurate model representation, (2) quick computation time of a schedule, and (3) clear communication of the model and the schedule.

the organization should be able to view and understand the model well enough to validate its structure, and once there is a schedule, it must be communicated to the organization. While a Gantt view is useful for showing sequences of tasks, it doesn't help anyone understand why the sequence makes sense or how it was chosen. A good solution improves not only the ability to create a schedule, but to visualize it and explain it across all levels of our organization.

First-generation simulation vs. Risk-based Planning and Scheduling (RPS)
In the first-generation simulation schedule tools, such as Preactor, the simulation model is deterministic and has a fixed model structure built into the system. Although the model framework is preset, a configuration file can be used to address issues like defining the number and type of workstations, the decision rules to apply within the model, the routing mechanism for jobs in the system, and the material constraints.

While providing a step forward, the first-generation simulation-based scheduling tools have two major shortcomings. First, as with other approaches to scheduling, the deterministic model of first-generation simulators means they must ignore variation, so they also generate optimistic schedules that can't always be met in the real system. And second, their fixed model structure limits their successful application to only simple systems. In essence, they focus on manufacturing applications where the factory is a standard job shop, where each job follows a fixed routing through the system, and each workstation may have a setup, processing, and teardown task. The model may also allow for secondary resources (like operators and tooling) to be specified for each of these tasks, while complex devices that handle materials (like conveyors, cranes, and automatic guided vehicles) are critical constraints that may not be included in the fixed job shop model. First-generation simulation-based scheduling tools, therefore, can only be applied to a subset of manufacturing applications, and have very limited application outside of this domain, including little use in transportation, logistics, or healthcare systems.

Simio's second-generation simulation-based scheduling approach is referred to as Risk-based Planning and Scheduling (RPS) and addresses the critical shortcomings of first-generation simulators by replacing the deterministic fixed model framework with a tailored stochastic simulation model built using a general simulation framework. This allows variation to be incorporated into the model, and for the constraints in the system to be fully modeled at any level of detail. By having a constraint model that captures all the critical constraints in the system, RPS systems can meet the objective of producing actionable schedules that can be executed in the real system, and account for variation and unplanned events.

So now, in the second section of this book, we will describe the details of the second-generation RPS approach, and how your company can reap its benefits and finally be able to fully deliver on your promises.

Simulation-Based Scheduling is Your Missing Piece

▶

···

CHAPTER 5

Everything You Need to Know about Risk-Based Planning and Scheduling (RPS)

Simio's Risk-based Planning and Scheduling (RPS) is the exciting next generation of APS that is based on a purpose-built simulation model of a company's system of operation. With the capabilities to fully capture detailed constraints and variations, RPS can account for risk and uncertainty, meaning it can address your scheduling needs in a way that all other approaches fail to do. In short, the RPS system creates and maintains the most accurate model representation, provides the quickest computation time for actionable schedules, and can clearly communicate the model structure and the resulting schedule to everyone who needs to know.

The most accurate model representation
One of the key advantages of RPS is its ability to flexibly define the constraint model used to generate the schedule. Although the first-generation simulation-based scheduling tools are an improvement over the constraint-based tools for capturing the operating constraints of the system, they are still limited in their

flexibility. In contrast, Simio's second-generation RPS approach removes all barriers in terms of flexibly modeling the system constraints. While the first-generation tools can be useful with relatively simple and well-structured applications, RPS's approach can be applied to a wide range of more complex systems. The flexibility of RPS also allows it to be used in a scheduler-in-the-loop environment, as well as a fully automated environment.

We will wait to address the nuts and bolts of creating the simulation model in the next chapter, and will instead leapfrog here to what the system can do with a model once it's completed. RPS initially uses the model in a purely deterministic mode, producing an idyllic scenario in which machines never break, process times are always constant, workers do not get sick, and materials arrive exactly on time. This is the optimistic view—the "happy" schedule we referred to earlier in the book—that is used as a baseline.

Once this schedule has been generated, RPS then uses the same simulation model but turns on variations to perform a probabilistic analysis to estimate the underlying risks associated with the schedule. In this analysis phase, RPS generates many different schedules based on random variations (like processing times that vary about their mean) and random events (where a machine breaks down). Similar to running a science experiment using specific controls while introducing certain variables, this analysis allows for an understanding of what occurs at different times in each replication of the schedule. The performance of each schedule is then measured across all replications using defined targets, such as on-time or on-cost delivery. The number of schedule replications with orders meeting those targets is then used to generate the likelihood that the target will be met.

The risk measures generated by RPS through this experimentation include the probability of meeting user-defined targets, as well as expected, pessimistic, and optimistic schedule performance. RPS still generates Gantt charts, except now those charts offer up far more data and become truly useful tools. The Gantt chart in Figure 13, for example, shows the likelihood of targets being met, along with color-coded bands based on the level of risk. A hover box shows planned, expected, pessimistic, and optimistic ship dates that are generated from the replicated simulation of the schedule generation.

Figure 13: The RPS Gantt includes color-coded risk measures.

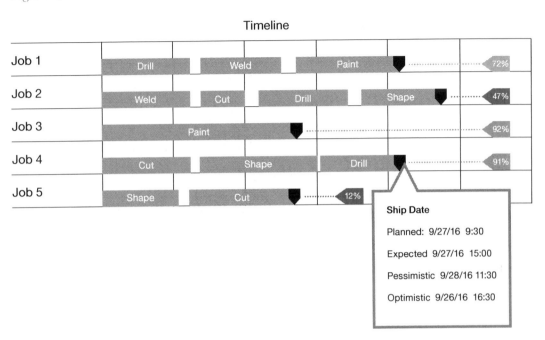

With the addition of the likelihood estimates and color-coded risk levels, the scheduler can quickly see that while orders #3 and #4 are okay, order #1 is a moderate risk, and #2 is a high risk. The scheduler can mitigate these risks by taking additional steps—whether that's scheduling overtime, splitting batches, or changing priorities—and comparing these alternatives and how they impact schedule targets and costs. As you can see here, RPS provides up-front visibility and a realistic view of expected schedule performance, allowing the scheduler to take preemptive actions and providing a customer-satisfying operational strategy at a minimum cost.

As an added bonus—something which first-generation simulators cannot do—the RPS model also allows a company to test the long-term impact of introducing a new product, adding a new piece of equipment, or making an additional process change based on a Lean Six Sigma project to reduce variation and improve performance. The multiple uses of the constraint model, for system design as well as for both real and hypothetical operation analysis, is a unique and invaluable feature of the RPS approach.

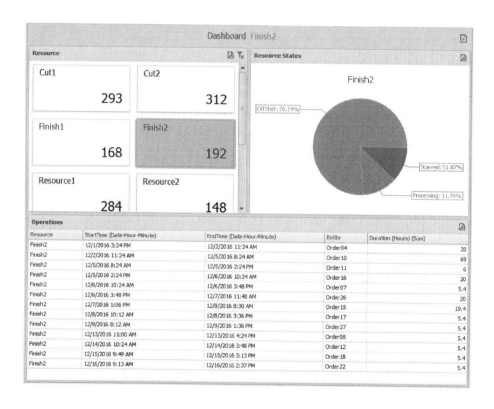

Figure 14: *This is a sample interactive dashboard generated from an RPS model that can be distributed via the cloud and displayed on touch-sensitive mobile devices to provide convenient access to scheduling results.*

The quickest computation time

RPS retains the speed advantage of the first-generation simulation-based tools without the disadvantage of a fixed constraint model. One of the biggest advantages, therefore, is RPS's extremely fast execution, allowing it to regenerate a schedule following an unplanned event. To repeat the metaphor mentioned in Chapter 4, RPS can provide the same immediate response that a driver gets when navigating with Google maps, because neither businesses nor drivers like to be lost.

To provide a framework that works in a scheduling environment, the RPS simulation engine automatically records detailed transactional data of all constraint-related actions in scheduling logs that can be viewed, filtered, and used for generating custom scheduling reports and dashboards. The data in these logs include information on materials, resources, orders, and material handling equipment, as well as non-value added time spent by orders constrained by the system. This information is invaluable for not only judging the quality of the schedule, but for also improving the schedule by providing both root cause information on schedule delays and development strategies for reducing non-value-added delays.

A flexible reporting engine allows this information to be captured in different ways and then distributed throughout the enterprise using the cloud [Figure 14].

The clearest communication

The benefits of RPS begin with its accurate and multi-purpose model and its quick computation time to generate an actionable schedule. But the benefits culminate in RPS's ability to communicate its structure, its model logic, and the resulting schedules to everyone who needs to know. And isn't this the most important element of all?

Like other scheduling tools, RPS provides both resource- and job-centric Gantt charts to show workflow through the system, and authorized users can drag and drop jobs on the resource Gantt chart and regenerate a schedule that reflects these changes in combination with the underlying model constraints. The RPS scheduling engine therefore simulates the flow of work based on the detailed model logic, while also respecting user drag-and-drop edits on the resource Gantt.

RPS also provides more operational insights over static Gantt charts through interactive 3D animation of the schedule, allowing users to preview a planned workflow. Detailed animation shows the movement of parts, workers, material-handling devices, and other critical constraints as the planned schedule unfolds. This animation can be helpful in understanding the underlying model, resolving any issues, and building confidence among the stakeholders.

Now that you understand the basic premise of Simio's Risk-based Planning and Scheduling model, we'll spend the next chapter detailing what it's like to actually implement this approach for your own company.

....

Figure 15: This is a snapshot of a Simio animation. To view an actual simulation, please visit www.simio.com

Implementing an RPS Scheduling Solution for Your Company

In this chapter, we'll walk you through the five steps needed to successfully implement a scheduling solution based on Simio's RPS approach. As you're reading, keep in mind that these steps are not always followed in an exact sequence, some steps can be taken concurrently, and several stages may have more than one iteration before an ideal solution unfolds. Also, we're keenly aware that each company has its own set of unique considerations, but this general framework can be used to understand a wide range of scheduling projects.

1. Identifying the key constraints in the system
2. Creating the data schema to drive the model
3. Creating the initial simulation model
4. Validating and enhancing the model
5. Training the users

#1: Identifying the key constraints in the system

To begin the implementation of RPS, it's necessary to understand the main constraints that must be incorporated into the simulation model. To clarify, a constraint is anything that may impede the flow of work through a system, resulting in a job spending unproductive time waiting for limited resources or materials. Because of such physical or logical constraints, it's not uncommon for a job to spend over 90 percent of its time in this "no-value" state.

Although constraints are unique to each system, the following are the four primary constraints in most systems.

* *Materials constraints:* Materials consumed or produced during the production process are a set of constraints. Materials that are produced in one area of a facility or in one location are typically consumed in another area or location. And in some cases, materials are linked to a specific job and must be reserved. This is considered another constraint.

* *Resource constraints:* Each resource that can limit the flow of work through the system—things like equipment, fixtures, or workers—is a constraint, but we do eliminate any inconsequential elements. If you always have plenty of pallets to move items between stations, for example, there's no reason to list pallets as a resource constraint. Are there complexities in your workforce that involve skills sets, learning curves, and special work rules? Those are the constraints we need to consider.

* *Buffer space and physical interference constraints:* A work area may accommodate up to four small components but only two large ones, for example. And if a crane needed to move a component is blocked by another crane, that would be a physical interference constraint.

* *Sequencing constraints:* This common constraint addresses issues of order. Do you have a paint booth that requires sequencing from light to dark? A rolling mill that requires sequencing from thick to thin? Jobs that need to be selected

so an oven can maintain a specified temperature range? When a job in your system is dependent on the job that precedes it, these are sequencing constraints that must be considered.

While these are the four primary constraint categories, other constraints may be unique to a system. When scheduling vessels for deliveries at offshore platforms, for example, there may be constraints on vessel movement based on the wind or wave heights. Fortunately, RPS is not restricted in the type and complexity of the constraints it can handle.

At this early stage, it's important to focus on those constraints that have a clear and direct impact on scheduling and not let extraneous details complicate the model. And while it's ideal if all critical constraints can be identified up front, RPS can remain flexible and allow the process to be iterative. Additional constraints can be added—and new constraints are often identified—throughout the implementation process, particularly as schedules are generated and the validation process begins.

A constraint is defined as anything that may impede the flow of work through a system. If constraints aren't recognized or handled properly, they can result in a job spending considerable time in a "no-value" state, which clearly affects the bottom line.

Figure 16: *Relational tables with cross-table references.*

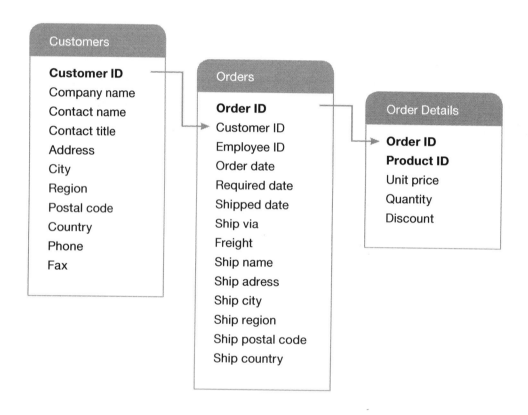

#2: Creating the data schema to drive the model

Once we have identified our initial set of constraints, our next step is to design the data tables that supply the relevant data to the simulation model. If we have resource constraints involving the skill levels of workers, for example, we need a data table that defines each worker and his or her skill, as well as related tables to define the schedules of those workers. Likewise, if we have a sequence constraint about a job setup and the job that follows, we need a corresponding table to define the data for the sequence-dependent setup times. This data schema also defines the work that must be done during the planning period, specifically a list of all jobs to be completed and the related data, including due date, priority, etc.

The data for a scheduling solution is typically held in relational tables, in which one row in a table references one or more rows in another table. For example, a customer record in the customer table references one or more orders in the order table, and each order references one or more records in the order details table [See Figure 16].

The number of tables and types of information held in these tables differs between applications. This design reflects the constraints of the model, as well as the sources and formats of the data that can be accessed in the ERP/APS/MES information systems. This data is typically imported from these information systems, as well as from spreadsheets and other data sources. It greatly simplifies the importation and implementation if the scheduling solution uses a data schema that matches the schema in these systems, so a first step is to leverage existing data schemas.

In some cases, the data schema for an implementation may follow the ISA 95 standard for representing manufacturing data, or it may be based on the Wonderware MES data model. This simplifies the project by allowing the associated data tables to be quickly and automatically generated using RPS tools. While the data schema may still need to be manually enhanced to reflect unique constraints, this provides a significant jumpstart on implementing a scheduling solution.

The next step is to establish data bindings for automatically importing data into the tables from existing sources, which allows the tables to be fully populated with data with a single mouse click. This data is frequently imported from the appropriate ERP/APS/MES sources, and is sometimes buffered by an intermediate data source. For example, when importing a list of manufacturing orders from SAP, the orders will first be exported from SAP to CSV or XML files before being imported into the scheduling solution. When direct links exist, it's possible to directly interface to data in MES systems, such as Wonderware.

We need to note here that a successful scheduling application very much depends on the quality of the data used to drive the model. The initial population of the scheduling data tables may reveal integrity issues with the data sources. And it's not uncommon to find errors or missing data; items in the products table, for example, are missing corresponding routings in the routings table. By validating such data early in the project, we can assure timely roll out of a new scheduling solution.

#3: Creating the initial simulation model

Once we have an initial data schema and sample data in place, we next focus on creating a first-cut simulation model that captures our constraints and references the data in our data tables. While we include as many of the critical constraints as possible, we can compromise some complexity in the interest of getting a working model running as quickly as possible.

In many applications, the first-cut simulation model can be automatically generated from the data in the data tables. RPS includes special tools and features that will automatically place resources such as machines and workers into the model, and incorporate additional constraints such as material requirements and sequence-dependent setup times. This ability to auto-generate the initial simulation model is part of a data-driven modeling approach and can dramatically reduce the implementation time for a project. This works particularly well when the data schema is patterned on the ISA 95 standard factory data model, or is based on the Wonderware MES data model. And the data-driven modeling approach is particularly powerful in applications where scheduling is being rolled out to many similar locations across the enterprise.

The data-driven modeling approach, however, does not work in all cases. In some applications, the system is unique and complex and the simulation model cannot be easily auto-generated from the data. In this situation, some clients already have a Simio simulation model of their system that they created to optimize their process design; we refer to this as the "design model" since it's helpful for analyzing and improving the existing system. We use this design model in conjunction with Lean Six Sigma or other process improvement methods to reduce variation and costs and to shorten lead times before moving on to the scheduling stage.

If a design model has not been built, then we have an opportunity to create a dual-use model that can be used for both design and scheduling. In some cases, the model allows for significant improvements in the system design, and it might make sense to initially focus on those process changes. In other cases, the process already runs well, but there are pressing needs to improve the day-to-day scheduling, and hence the initial focus will rest there. Regardless of where we start, however, the simulation model can support both design and scheduling, which is a compelling advantage of the RPS approach.

Whether we're using a data-driven modeling approach, leveraging an existing design model, or building a new simulation model from scratch, our initial goal is to get a working solution. Part of this first-cut simulation modeling effort may also involve creating customer reports and dashboards for viewing the schedule, as well as scheduling rules for selecting between jobs to process next, or when assigning a job to one or more available resources. However, in most cases the first-cut simulation model will use standard available reports/dashboards and scheduling rules in the interest of getting a working first-cut solution.

Finally, for reasons emphasized in this book, it's important to incorporate variation and unplanned events into the simulation model. Setup and processing times, for example, should not be considered exact, and machines should encounter interruptions due to jams or breakdowns just like they would in the real system. Although you may not have all the information on process variation, you can still make assumptions to factor variation into the model, and then refine these assumptions as you get more information. Each processing time can be represented as a triangular distribution, for example, where the most likely value is specified by the ERP-provided processing time, but a maximum and minimum processing time is specified as percentage above and below this value.

#4: Validating and enhancing the simulation model

Experience shows that using an iterative approach to simulation modeling—in which you start with a basic model and enhance it over time—is the best strategy for determining the appropriate level of detail in the simulation model. Once we have a working model and can generate an actual schedule, we begin the process of enhancing the model, whether that's adding more constraint logic or more powerful decision rules to make smarter decisions when selecting jobs and assigning resources. Again, it's critical to see this as a process where we make incremental improvements to the model until the resulting schedules satisfy all critical constraints, are fully actionable, and produce good KPIs.

The validation process focuses on both the model structure and the schedule outputs. So, as we add each level of enhancements to the model, we test the resulting schedule by asking the following key questions:

- Is the schedule actionable? If not, we define the key constraints that are being violated and add logic to the model to represent these constraints.
- Are there still improvements that could be made to the schedule to enhance our KPIs? If so, we enhance our decision logic to improve selection.

One of the best ways to validate the model structure is to view 3D animations of the schedule generation process, because it gives a powerful visualization of the constraint logic. The validation team should certainly include the schedulers, but it should also involve operators on the floor who are accustomed to making on-the-fly adjustments to the schedules they receive. As with any plan, the best-case scenario is when everyone understands—from the front line to the executives—the why and how as well as the what of the schedule.

During this enhancement phase, we also expand the number of data sets we're running through the model. We eventually cut over to using actual data that is updated at the beginning of each shift, and compare our generated schedules to the actual schedules that are being executed. And we continually compare the quality of our generated schedules to the existing scheduling system, which is often a manual approach.

As we refine our decision logic in the model, we use the features of RPS to run experiments to see the impact of adopting different decision rules within the scheduling logic. For example, we might have a bottleneck resource with sequence-dependent setup times, and we're using a minimum changeover rule for selecting the next job. So, we use the experimentation feature to refine this decision based on different tie-breaking rules (earliest due date versus smallest remaining slack, for example). These experimentations also allow us to evaluate look-ahead windows where we only consider jobs that fall within that window. This provides a rigorous basis for refining and improving the decision rules.

The enhancement and validation phase continues until there are small, diminishing returns from further enhancements. At this point the system is ready to go live, but keep in mind that further enhancements can be made as we learn from use in the actual scheduling environment.

#5: Training the users

Once the validation phase is over and the system can go live, the next step is to train those involved. This should include not only the mechanics of how to generate a schedule and interpret results, but also an understanding of the constraint model and how the system works. Proper training is a critical step in ensuring that everyone involved can fully leverage the power of the new scheduling system.

It's important to note that the most effective training occurs when the end users of the solution have been involved in its implementation from the start. People who use the reports and dashboards from the system should have input in their design, and those who work to implement the schedule should be part of the refinement and validation process. If this occurs, by the time final training begins, there's already familiarity and buy-in to the solution—along with a sense of relief that scheduling headaches are over!

The final section of *Deliver on Your Promise* offers up some case studies so you can see for yourself the kind of success that can come from implementing an RPS system for your company.

Risk-based Planning and Scheduling in the 4th Industrial Revolution

Imagine a production system where all production decisions are optimized based on real time information from a fully integrated and connected set of equipment and people. The entire system makes the best possible use of the available resources to achieve its production goals, and the system automatically adjusts in real time to changing conditions. All work is automatically scheduled through the system, and all equipment automatically records their performance and plans and schedules their own maintenance to minimize impact on the system. Performance data is automatically recorded throughout the system, and reported to the appropriate stakeholders. In addition, the system projects forward in time and provides reliable management information on planned performance including critical KPIs such as expected delivery time and production costs for all planned orders. Managers have instant access to both current and important forward-looking information to drive and grow the business. This is the vision of the Smart Factory of the future.

The Smart Factory is referred to as the 4th industrial revolution, and Industry 4.0 is a common name used to describe the current trend towards a fully connected and automated production system. This term originates from a project in the high-tech strategy of the German government, and Figure 17 depicts the four industrial revolutions. The first is the introduction of mechanization and power to reduce reliance on humans. The second is the introduction of mass production, assembly lines, and electricity to dramatically improve production efficiency. The third is the introduction of computers and automation to control individual machines and help plan production. The fourth is the concept of cyber-physical systems where the components are fully connected, monitored, and interfaced to a virtual model of the system to predict and improve the performance of the system.

The Industry 4.0 initiative is driven by four key design principles. The first design principle is the interoperability of components and data. In the Smart Factory, machines, devices, sensors, and people connect and communicate with each other via the Internet of Things (IoT). A second design principle is information transparency where real time sensor data is connected to the virtual factory model. This provides system-wide visibility of the factory status along with higher-value context information. A third design principle is technical assistance. This includes decision support systems to solve urgent problems on short notice (e.g. rescheduling after a machine breakdown). It also includes the aggregations and visualization of data to support continuous improvement in the production process. The fourth design principle is decentralized decisions. This refers to the components of the system being able to perform as many tasks as autonomously as possible. For example, machines that self-diagnose to detect out of limit operations and request repair.

The interconnected components of the Smart Factory automatically record detailed performance data that can be stored and analyzed to fine tune and improve the system performance. Data analytics can be applied to this information to discover and communicate meaningful data patterns and trends. Although data analytics applied to past data is useful, the real power comes from connecting the real-time component data to the virtual model of the factory. The model can then be used to project forward in time and reveal and address problems and issues

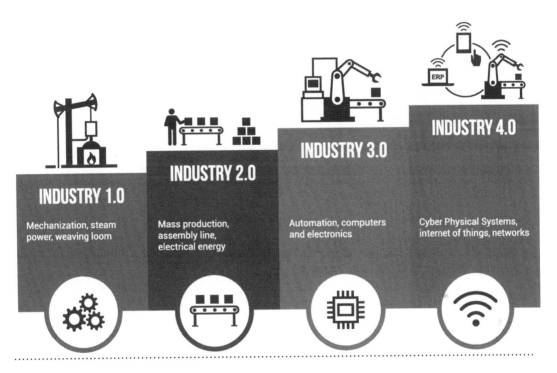

Figure 17: *The four industrial revolutions.*

in the production plan before they occur in the real system. The virtual factory model ("digital twin") is a key component of the Smart Factory of the future. It provides both a system-wide aggregated view of the state of the production system, as well as a means of projecting forward in time to see the expected future state.

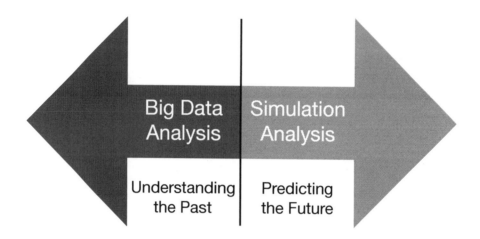

Simio's RPS modeling system is designed to provide the virtual factory model for the Smart Factory of the future. RPS differs from traditional simulation modeling tools in that is designed from the ground up to execute as a live component of a factory execution system. RPS differs from traditional manufacturing modeling systems in that it supports complex in-memory relational data, connections to real time data sources, complex dynamic decision rules, detailed resource, material, and task logging, along with customizable Gantts, reports, and dashboards for communicating scheduling results. This is essential functionality for providing a connected virtual factory model in a Smart Factory.

As discussed in Chapter 4, traditional scheduling tools are inadequate for capturing the detailed constraint model of many manufacturing systems. As a second-generation simulation-based scheduling tool, Simio RPS can flexibly model all the critical constraints of the factory, so that the resulting schedules reflect the true constraints of the system. This is essential to support automated scheduling and rescheduling in the Smart Factory of the future. The predictive power of the model is only valuable when the true constraints of the system are captured in the factory model; otherwise the projections from the model are invalid and typically over promise since they ignore important constraints that are present in the real system.

As discussed in Chapter 3, variation and unplanned events have a significant impact on system performance. Therefore, it is essential that any deterministic schedule that is generated by the factory model be viewed as optimistic. A deterministic schedule assumes that everything goes exactly as planned. Unplanned events (e.g. breakdowns, staffing/material shortages, etc.) and variations in times degrade the actual performance. Hence the factory model must incorporate this uncertainty to assess the risk associated with a specific schedule. Simio's RPS provides for both the generation of a deterministic schedule as well as analysis of the associated risk for the schedule using a single factory model.

By enabling both the generation of a detailed factory schedule based on an accurate constraint model of the system, and risk assessment of that schedule base on uncertainty, the Smart Factory of the future has the forward visibility to reduce risks for meeting important KPIs such as on time delivery of products. The impact and cost of tactical decisions such as overtime or expediting materials for migrating delivery risks can be quickly and easily assessed using the factory model.

Simio's RPS modeling system is designed to provide the virtual factory model for the Smart Factory of the future.

A key enabling technology for the Smart Factory of the future is the interconnectivity of the components of the system. This allows for sharing of data and system state throughout the system. To fully leverage this power, the factory model must be fully integrated and connected to this live data. This data is often complex, relational, and changes dynamically as events occur on the factory floor. Simio RPS is specifically designed to operate in this dynamic data environment.

Figure 18 depicts the relationship of the virtual factory model to the ERP and MES/IoT, along with the key capabilities that are enabled in the Smart Factory by the virtual factory model. It's only by using this model that the system can project forward in time and support the identification and resolution of issues before they arise in the real system. Interconnectivity between the ERP, MES/IoT, and the virtual factory model are key enablers of this capability.

The basic idea of the Smart Factory goes back to the 1980s, when many of the necessary components were becoming reality. The introduction of robots, automatic guided vehicles, manufacturing execution systems, data analytics, and information networks created the promise of the "lights-out" factory where the system runs efficiently with little or no human intervention. The move towards a lights-out factory was led in the 1980s by the American automotive companies as part of an initiative to radically change manufacturing to compete with the Japanese car makers. However, manufacturing revolutions never happen overnight and the move to a lights-out factory was more challenging than envisioned. Most of the Smart Factories of the past were demonstration or proof-of-concept sites and the mainstream shift to the 4th-generation industry has yet to fully materialize. Japan's advantage, it turned out, lay more in people-based lean manufacturing than in automation. The Smart Factory makes use of automation, but does not place full automation at the center of its vision.

The Smart Factory is an idea whose time has come. The technologies underpinning the Smart Factory have continued to evolve and become more mainstream. Each piece is familiar technology, and is in place in many factories today. However, the detailed factory model to provide forward visibility into the planned operations, supporting ongoing continuous improvement initiatives, has been a key missing component. Simio RPS provides this critical component.

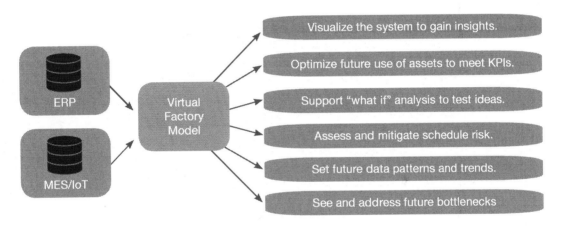

Figure 18: The relationship of the virtual factory model to the ERP and MES/IoT.

RPS Success Stories

....

RPS Success Stories

Because of the underlying flexibility of the RPS model, we've seen successful applications in many areas, including manufacturing, logistics, and healthcare. In this section, we'll briefly describe examples of complex scheduling applications in each of these areas based on the RPS approach described in this book.

Before going further, however, we should point out that for several reasons—mainly competition—many customers are reluctant to provide detailed information on their successful Simio RPS applications. Because good scheduling provides such a competitive edge, companies aren't always willing to readily share their success. In fact, the more successful the project is in terms of on-time and on-cost delivery, the more incentive an enterprise has to remain quiet on how scheduling impacted their bottom line performance! And while we'd like to be able to quote specific KPI enhancements (such as impact on revenue, cost, on-time delivery, and throughput), these aren't numbers that customers are typically willing to share. We can state for the record, however, that we have customers that have internally documented hundreds of millions of dollars of annual savings using Simio RPS.

In the following pages, we'll present a handful of successful applications of Simio's RPS, including a company that supplies medical materials to a network of state-of-the-art hospitals in Denmark to a manufacturing application that put our system to the ultimate test.

We can state for the record that we have customers that have internally documented hundreds of millions of dollars of annual savings using Simio RPS.

BAE Systems

Manufacturing

As a defense contractor, BAE Systems must reliably plan and predict production resources to meet the military's needs—on-time delivery and within budget. What their managers needed was more effective methods for production resource risk mitigation.

BAE Systems used Simio's RPS solution to provide planners and schedulers with a customized interface for generating schedules, performing risk and cost analysis, investigating potential improvements, and viewing 3D animations. Gantt charts now make it easy for their managers to see the timing of processes and to explore how changes in equipment or employees affect that timing. BAE Systems can run additional simulations whenever one or more factors change, resulting in a "finger on the pulse" awareness that allows quick adjustments and assures confident decision making.

Simio's RPS helps BAE Systems meet production deadlines and is now used for a variety of forecasting and scheduling challenges including decreasing overtime, managing equipment reliability issues, developing training goals, writing proposals, and evaluating capital investments.

John Deere Cast Iron Foundry

Manufacturing

Simio's RPS was implemented to improve the production scheduling at the John Deere Cast Iron Foundry in Waterloo Iowa. Many industries demand complex sequencing that involves multiple constraints in order to find the most feasible production schedule. This is particularly true for the highly automated and complex John Deere Cast Iron Foundry, which produces several hundred parts with various iron recipes and production constraints. The challenge was to have an integrated production scheduling system that allows for real-time data exchange between the Wonderware MES, and SAP ERP, as well as a system that could create a schedule based on the actual status of the production line with complex production constraints. The solution was implemented using Simio's RPS, and it has allowed us to consider complex material requirements, equipment resource availability, due dates, and nine different sequencing constraints.'

John Deere has not published a case study on this application, but this description is a summary of the presentation abstract, approved by John Deere, for Simulation-Based Scheduling at John Deere, which was given at the 2015 IIE Annual Conference and Expo in Anaheim, California.

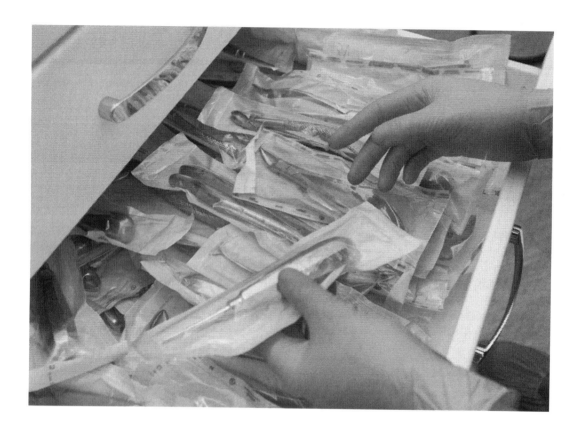

Capital Region of Denmark

Healthcare

The health system in the Capital Region of Denmark is a world-class automated health system that includes two Central Sterile Services Departments (CSSD), and two distribution centers that handle the receipt and dispatch of goods for the two CSSDs.

The CSSDs and distribution centers are automated by robots for loading and unloading of storage goods and AGVs. Besides the transport of sterile goods, the distribution centers also handle other goods such as medicine, linen, uniforms, and waste. The CSSDs also supply other hospitals in the system with surgical equipment, ensuring the right equipment will be in the right place at the start of each day.

From the goods receipt, SAP system, or the sterile system, the MES system (which is Wonderware) receives information about items in the distribution center that must either be delivered within the hospital or sent by external transport to additional hospitals.

Planning and scheduling of all transports is done using Simio's RPS, which directly integrates with the Wonderware MES system. The schedule considers the type of object that must be transported, the expected transport time, and the capacity constraints in the facilities. The RPS module creates an optimized plan for execution that is based on the simulated model of the system. Scheduling and re-scheduling is carried out automatically in response to events, and it reflects the current load of the facility.

Shell Gulf of Mexico

Logistics

Shell Gulf of Mexico moves more than 50,000 tons of materials and equipment to offshore facilities each month using more than 40 offshore supply vessels. The shipments are broken into voyages, which include loading of the vessel, transiting to offshore locations, transferring materials offshore, returning to port, unloading, and possibly tank cleaning. In a typical month, Shell will schedule over 200 voyages that transport more than 9,000 tracked items—anything from a simple pallet of chemicals to 20,000 feet of tubular goods.

The offshore supply vessels employed come in a variety of sizes and configurations: the vessels range in length from 100 to over 350 feet, with cargo capacities ranging from 500 to 6,000 tons. Open back deck areas and below deck storage vary in terms of capacities and types of storage. Vessel travel durations are determined based on the distance between the port and rigs, and the travel rate of the vessel is dependent upon weather and location.

The complex scheduling process revolves around shipping requests, which identify the materials and equipment that need to be shipped within the next 5 to 10 days. Requests include the pickup and delivery points, quantities, dimensions, weights, and time constraints. Each port has a number of loading, unloading, and tank cleaning slips, and information about the slips' capabilities, vessel capacity, selection ranking, and load and unload times are configured for each slip.

Because of the enormity of the system and the presence of so much variability, Shell selected Simio's RPS for the solution. The RPS has allowed Shell to generate schedules that meet their complex constraints, and to assess the risk associated with the schedules. The results from RPS are displayed in Gantt charts that visually display the details of each rig, slip, vessel, and demand item, and customized reports and dashboards are used to view the schedule from different perspectives.

Glossary

Actionable schedule: a detailed schedule of work that explicitly considers all relevant resource, material, sequence, and other constraints in the system, and can therefore be executed in the real system.

Advanced Planning and Optimization (APO): another name for the Advanced Planning and Scheduling (APS) module of an Enterprise Resource Planning (ERP) system. The SAP module, for example, is called APO.

Advanced Planning and Scheduling (APS): a tool that adds supply chain planning and scheduling capabilities to the Enterprise Resource Planning system. APS sometimes includes detailed production scheduling using a constraint-based or first generation simulation-based approach.

Backward scheduling: a method to determine a master production plan by working backwards from a due date to a start date. Backward scheduling is typically done using fixed time buckets or planning periods, and is based on the assumption of a constant lead time and infinite capacity and then computing the associated material requirements.

Bill of Material (BOM): a hierarchical list of raw materials, component parts, and sub-assemblies required to produce a product. The BOM is required by a scheduling system to schedule demand based on both material requirements and capacity.

Constraint model: a scheduling model that includes resource, material, logic, sequencing, and other constraints in a system. If the constraint model captures all the critical constraints, the resulting schedule is actionable. Otherwise, the schedule cannot be executed in the real system due to the missing constraints.

Constraint Programming (CP): a constraint modeling technique where relations between variables are stated in the form of constraints, often expressed as mathematical equations (or inequalities). A solution to the constraint set is found using a heuristic solver. Special constraint forms allow this approach to be applied to some scheduling problems. This approach is limited in flexibility and can require long computation times.

Deterministic process: a process with no variation or unplanned events. A system without variation performs significantly better than the same system with variation.

Dispatching rule: an algorithm for deciding which job to process next in a production facility, such as which job has the earliest due date or which requires a minimum changeover.

Enterprise Resource Planning (ERP): enhancements of the original Material Requirements Planning (MRP) functions in order to bring together accounting, human resources, and other functions into a fully integrated IT system. ERP also incorporated Supply Chain Management (SCM) to extend inventory control over a broader scope, including distribution.

Exponential distribution: a probability distribution that describes the time between events in a process (called a Poisson process) where the events occur independently and continuously at a constant average rate. This distribution is commonly used to model random arrivals, but is typically not appropriate for modeling task times.

Finite Capacity Scheduling (FCS): a scheduling approach that accounts for the limited production capacity of the system. This contrasts with the Enterprise Resource Planning system that typically assumes an infinite capacity.

First generation simulation-based scheduling: a scheduling approach based on a deterministic and fixed simulation model that is configured using one or more data files. These tools are generally more flexible than constraint-based approaches and execute faster, but because their underlying model structure is fixed, they can't be used in many complex applications.

Gantt chart: a chart used in scheduling applications for showing activities over a timeline. A resource Gantt and an entity Gantt show the same information, but from two different perspectives.

Heuristic rule: a method for problem solving based on a practical approach. The approach is not guaranteed to be optimal or perfect, but it is useful for meeting immediate goals.

Industry 4.0 (Smart Factory): a common name used to describe the current trend towards a fully connected and automated production system, also referred to as the Smart Factory. This term originates from a project in the high-tech strategy of the German government.

Lead time: the duration from the start of physical production to the completion of the production process. The lead times defined by an ERP system, which is based on backward scheduling, is often substantially shorter than actual lead times in production.

Lean Manufacturing: a systematic method derived from the Toyota Production System for the elimination of waste within a production system. Lean manufacturing is often associated with the term Muda, a Japanese word meaning "wastefulness."

Manufacturing Execution System (MES): a computerized system used to track and document the transformation or raw materials into finished goods, including the status of resources and the flow of work.

Material Requirements Planning (MRP): a system developed by Joe Orlicky that helps manufacturers plan their purchasing and production activities, assuming fixed lead times and an infinite capacity.

NP-hard: complex problems in computational complexity theory that are classified as "non-deterministic polynomial-time hard." The job-shop scheduling problem is a well-known NP-hard problem.

Planning: the high-level process of creating a master production plan by identifying what work needs to be done, what materials are required to perform that work, and where the work will take place. Planning is typically followed by scheduling, which focuses more on the "how" of the production.

Risk Based Planning and Scheduling (RPS): the use of a custom-built stochastic simulation model for both system design and scheduling. RPS incorporates risk measures for assessing the robustness of a production schedule.

Scheduling: the process of turning a master production plan into a detailed, actionable schedule that can be followed to produce required items while meeting key objectives. Scheduling requires a detailed model of all the critical constraints in a system, and a good schedule is dependent upon good planning.

Simulation: the imitation of the operation of a system or process over time. Simulation is done with a model of a system, one that represents the key constraints, characteristics, or behaviors of that system.

Six Sigma: A process improvement methodology introduced at Motorola that focuses on identifying and removing defects and minimizing variation.

Smart Factory (Industry 4.0): a name given to the fully connected and automated production system, based on digital part data, interconnected devices, and a virtual factory model to plan and project the future of products and production facilities. The Industry 4.0 initiative is focused on creating the Smart Factory of the future.

Supervisory Control and Data Acquisition (SCADA): a control system architecture that uses programmable logic controllers, networked data communications, and graphical user interfaces for high-level process supervisory management of production equipment.

Supply Chain Management (SCM): the management of the flow of goods and services from raw materials to finished products, from the point of origin to the point of consumption.

Variation: routine deviations that occur in processes that become a primary driver of poor performance in any manufacturing process. Any schedule that is generated without accounting for variation is optimistic and over promises.

Acknowledgements

I would like to thank the many people who've contributed to the ideas presented in this book. That list would be far too long to include here, but I offer my gratitude to all those who've influenced my work and helped shape these ideas over time.

Special thanks to those who reviewed the early drafts and made suggestions for improvements, including the team at Simio LLC, most notably Rich Ritchie, Dave Sturrock, Gerrit Zaayman, Renee Thiesing, Glen Wirth, Anthony Innamorato, and Eric Howard. Several people outside Simio also provided valuable feedback, including Heinz Weigl, Pricha Pantumsinchai, Shawn Snapp, Erick Wikum, Ricki Ingalls, Greg Quinn, and Gregory J. Lynch.

Deep appreciation to the simulation and scheduling teams at Simio LLC for designing and implementing the second generation Simio Risk-Based Planning and Scheduling tool that is touted in this book. They are an exceptionally talented and dedicated team of individuals, and they continue to evolve and advance this exciting new technology.

Finally, I would like to thank Clew Publishing for the editing and layout work that transformed the initial manuscript into this final version.

Made in the USA
Lexington, KY
07 November 2017